Letters on God
and
Letters to a Young Woman

NORTHWESTERN WORLD CLASSICS

Northwestern World Classics brings readers
the world's greatest literature. The series features
essential new editions of well-known works,
lesser-known books that merit reconsideration,
and lost classics of fiction, drama, and poetry.
Insightful commentary and compelling new translations
help readers discover the joy of outstanding writing
from all regions of the world.

Rainer Maria Rilke

Letters on God
and Letters to a
Young Woman

Translated from the German
by Annemarie S. Kidder

Northwestern University Press ✦ *Evanston, Illinois*

Northwestern University Press
www.nupress.northwestern.edu

English translation, introductory material, and notes copyright © 2012 by Annemarie S. Kidder. Published 2012 by Northwestern University Press. *Letters on God* originally published in German by Insel-Verlag under the title *Über Gott,* copyright © 1933 by Insel-Verlag, Leipzig. *Letters to a Young Woman* originally published in German by Insel-Verlag under the title *Briefe an eine junge Frau,* copyright © 1930 by Insel-Verlag, Leipzig. All rights reserved.

Printed in the United States of America

10 9 8 7 6 5 4 3 2 1

Library of Congress Cataloging-in-Publication Data

Rilke, Rainer Maria, 1875–1926.
  [Über Gott. English]
  Letters on God ; and, Letters to a young woman / Rainer Maria Rilke ; translated from the German by Annemarie S. Kidder.
    p. cm. — (Northwestern world classics)
  "Letters on God originally published in German by Insel-Verlag under the title Über Gott, copyright © 1933 by Insel-Verlag, Leipzig. Letters to a Young Woman originally published in German by Insel-Verlag under the title Briefe an eine junge Frau, copyright © 1930 by Insel-Verlag, Leipzig."—T.p. verso.
  Includes bibliographical references.
  ISBN 978-0-8101-2740-1 (pbk. : alk. paper)
  1. Rilke, Rainer Maria, 1875–1926—Correspondence. 2. Rilke, Rainer Maria, 1875–1926—Translations into English. 3. Authors, German—20th century—Correspondence. I. Kidder, Annemarie S. II. Rilke, Rainer Maria, 1875–1926. Briefe an eine junge Frau. English. III. Title. IV. Series: Northwestern world classics.
PT2635.I65A2 2012
831.912—dc23

                                          2012000888

∞ The paper used in this publication meets the minimum requirements of the American National Standard for Information Sciences—Permanence of Paper for Printed Library Materials, ANSI Z39.48-1992.

CONTENTS

For the first time, this volume makes available to an English-speaking audience two of the earliest collections of letters written by Rainer Maria Rilke (1875–1926) and published after his death: one on the theme of God, the other addressed to a young woman. *Letters on God* has never before been translated into English in book form. *Letters to a Young Woman* was translated into English by K. W. Maurer in 1945, shortly after World War II, but the book has been out of print for half a century.

Rilke was an avid letter writer, and more than seven thousand of his letters have survived. Carefully composed on stationery with printed letterhead and a copy made for his own files, they often were sent via registered mail in an envelope that bore Rilke's personal waxed seal. Recipients were friends and family, novelists and poets, painters and sculptors, literary critics and publishers, and those who upon reading his work had contacted the poet and counted themselves among his admirers. The best-known collection today is *Letters to a Young Poet.* Their recipient was one such admirer, Franz Xaver Kappus, who had sought the poet's help in refining his own poetic ambitions. These letters were among the first published after Rilke's death.

In 1927, Rilke's daughter, Ruth Rilke-Sieber, and son-in-law, Carl Sieber, gathered, cataloged, and edited the mountain of Rilke correspondence. In 1929, the first chronological collection of Rilke letters appeared, covering the years from 1902 to 1906, followed by five more volumes, all organized by chronology. Between 1929 and 1939, the Siebers saw to the chronological editions of six volumes of Rilke letters, and they reissued and expanded another six-volume edition published between 1936 and 1939. Over time, Rilke's letters were collected and published according to four categories: letters collected by chronology; letters organized by themes—such as the arts, poetry, and politics; letters sent to a certain person; and letters sent to and received from a particular person.

The earliest editions of Rilke letters contained those sent to one person. The first collection was published in 1927 by the letters' recipient, comprising six letters from the last year of Rilke's life to the Dutch publisher Alexander Alphons Marius Stols. Two more collections appeared in 1928: one by the French Rilke biographer Maurice Betz, containing three letters Rilke had sent him, the other a set of letters that Rilke had sent to Auguste Rodin (1840–1917). In 1929, the Siebers issued their first volume of Rilke letters addressed to one person. The *Letters to a Young Poet* (*Briefe an einen jungen Dichter*) contains ten letters to Kappus spanning largely two years (1903–4, with one letter written in 1908) and an introduction by the "young poet" Kappus himself. A similar collection appeared the following year. Titled *Letters to a Young Woman* (*Briefe an eine junge Frau*), this 1930 volume contains nine letters to Lisa Heise and a brief epilogue by Carl Sieber. In 1934, Heise published the letters she had sent to Rilke. (In 2003, Insel Verlag issued a German edition containing both sets of correspondence between Heise and Rilke. Edited and with a commentary by Horst Nalewski, this edition also contains a previously unpublished 1924 Rilke letter, his last to her, and a biographical sketch of Heise with autobiographical notes, literary excerpts, and photographs.)

Also from this early stage of the publication of Rilke letters comes a collection focusing on one particular theme. The first thematic collection was published in 1933 and is titled *On God: Two Letters* (*Über Gott: Zwei Briefe;* it was reissued in German by Insel Verlag in 1996). It contains the two letters and an introduction by Carl Sieber. Since Rilke's thematic reflections in *On God* offer a framework through which to read even his preceding correspondence, that volume is presented here first.

Letters on God

Rilke was driven by what could be called a quest for God. Even a cursory reading of Rilke's poetry reveals that a prominent theme of his is the heart's insatiable longing after the transcendent, the divine. This theme is variably approached and expressed through the use of images borrowed from the Christian tradition and Greek mythology. God and nature, prayer and longing, an ethics of love and a passion for life all find their way into Rilke's poetry and raise the perennial question about the nature of people's relationship with the transcendent other. Rilke grapples with the person and the nature of God most explicitly in *The Book of Hours* (*Das Stundenbuch*). Published in 1905, *The Book of Hours* is regarded as Rilke's first significant literary contribution. A tripartite work containing the "Book of the Monkish Life," the "Book of Pilgrimage," and the "Book of Poverty and Death," it is a series of prayers written as if by a Russian monk turned iconographer. Rilke had insisted that these prayers were not to be read as separate poems but as one long continuous prayer, divided into three parts. In them, God is viewed as evolving progressively and gradually, while remaining concealed to those who are looking for him mostly within the church and the confines of ecclesiastical tradition.

In Rilke's *Book of Hours,* God hides in the ordinary, in the easily overlooked, in the world of concrete objects in nature, in the core of the person's interior. Instead of regarding God as clothed in glorious splendor, victorious might, and heavenly light in accordance with traditional church teachings, Rilke views him as concealed in lowliness and poverty, hidden within the smallest crevices of the human heart and the soul's dark night. It is up to the individual, says Rilke, to recover God's felt presence and his sovereignty in all of creation. When thus focused, one will become a co-laborer with God in the gradual process of transforming creation. The responsibility of recovering God's presence in life does not fall to the church's office bearers and to priests but to artists and poets, painters and sculptors. For Rilke, the artist's role is that of priest and mediator between people, God, and creation. His or her responsibilities will entail the close observation of nature, intensive work, and diligent concentration. Creating an object of art will mean the kind of labor that lacks public recognition and applause. The artist should be prepared to suffer and seek solitude for the sake of the craft and sacrifice personal attachments and the comforts of a stable career. The artist will have served God well when the object of art is capable of allowing people to discover God by means of it. On his part, Rilke had given up steady employment, his marriage, and family life to fully devote himself to the art of poetry and writing. In formulating his views on God and the role of the artist as priest and mediator, Rilke drew inspiration from lectures on art and religion he had attended at the Universities of Munich and Berlin, his travels through Russia and Italy, his close observation of the sculptor Auguste Rodin in his Paris studio, and his numerous visits to churches, monasteries, museums, and sacred sites in Russia, Italy, and France.

Rilke's views on God were shaped by his Roman Catholic upbringing. The spiritual writer and Trappist monk Thomas Merton says that Rilke was "a typical witness of a certain type of modern religious consciousness. He was not 'godless.' His heritage was profoundly Catholic and yet like so many of his contemporaries he found much that he could not accept in ordinary Catholic belief and practice," so that "his poetic consciousness adopted a symbolic and spiritual idea of historic cycles in religious vitality." These cycles, according to Merton, find God first in simplicity, then in building temples for God, and then, upon finding these temples empty and nearly destroyed, in a renewed God search and in people's "creative effort" that would allow the God of history to become once more manifest and "the cosmos once more 'transparent.'" As a child, Rilke had been exposed to his mother's religious zeal and fervent Catholic piety. About Rilke's mother, Sophia "Phia" Rilke, Hertha Koenig says in her memoir that "the close ties with her Catholic church were so strongly apparent that one almost felt it indecorous to sit next to this woman in an earthly sphere and to have other than pious thoughts." As an adult, Rilke rejects such ostentatious piety as grotesque, superficial, and meaningless. In its place he seeks to formulate an inward piety, or an existential wisdom for life, that is at times modeled after the life of the saints and monastics in their direct and open dialogue with God in prayer. In this God search, Rilke makes use of the religious artwork in the churches of the East and West and the regular, lifelong reading of a leatherbound Luther edition of the Bible with Apocrypha.

The imagery Rilke employs in his poetry comes both from the Bible and Greek mythology. Consequently, Rilke has no problem alternating between the words "God" or "gods" when describing or alluding to transcendent reality and ultimate truth. Rilke's God does not easily align with traditional church doctrine. Rather, his view of God is experiential; it cannot be separated from life in the here and now, the human body, the things in the world, or nature. Only by concentrating on and accepting what exists in the visible and finite world can one come to perceive the invisible and infinite. For Rilke, a search for God by means of shortcuts into the otherworldly, into heavenly bliss, into the life beyond is a betrayal of God's nature and creation, a gross misinterpretation of Jesus Christ's teachings, a misunderstanding of the role of Christ today and the mystery of earthly life.

In addition to *The Book of Hours,* Rilke completed two other books of poems with an explicitly Christian theme. The first is *The Visions of Christ* (*Die Christusvisionen*), which he refused to have published during his lifetime. The *Visions* contains eleven narrative poems on the role of Christ as a teacher and his earthly ministry in a contemporary setting. They were composed in two stages: the first between October 1896 and 1897 in Munich, where in 1897 Rilke was attending lectures on art history, philosophy, and religion at the University of Munich; the second in July 1898 in Zoppot on the Baltic Sea, where he wrote three more poems. All eleven poems depict Christ as eternal wanderer and his physical and spiritual appearance in the modern world. In most of the scenes, he is faced with the results of his teachings or, more frequently, their distortion by his followers.

Initially Rilke had been enthusiastic about the publication of the Christ poems. In an 1897 letter to Karl Baron Du Prel, a philosopher and student of spiritualism, Rilke had affirmed the power of the spiritual over the material: "Every artist must struggle through the misty fumes of crass materialism toward those spiritual intimations that build for him the golden bridge into shoreless eternities." Rilke had hoped to "become with word and pen one of the adherents of the new faith that towers high above church steeple crosses," so that by *The Visions of Christ,* slated for publication that same year, "I shall come a big step nearer to your group." Though the Christ poems were not published as planned in the periodical *Society* (*Die Gesellschaft*), its editor, Michael Conrad, played a role in helping Rilke clarify his view on Christ when pointing him to an article titled "Jesus the Jew" ("Jesus der Jude"), which revealed similarities with Rilke's own position. Rilke was eager to meet its author, Lou Andreas-Salomé, a noted philosophical essayist, novelist, and literary critic, with whom he could readily agree on several of her conclusions about Jesus. Prominent among them was that only the loner, like Christ, "reaches the heights of religion, its true bliss and fullest tragedy; what he experiences there escapes the crowd below; his tragic end and his tragic perception remain as mysterious and individualistic as his inspiration and oneness with God—they belong outside of history." Furthermore, she suggested that religious experience achieves validity only in living, feeling, and emphatically suffering God solely through the emotions. In his first letter to her of May 13, 1897, Rilke recounts the essay's impact on him: "Your essay related to my [Christ] poems like dream to reality, like a wish to its fulfillment." Eventually, she would become his lover and, after their break in 1901 and Rilke's marriage to Clara Westhoff the same year, continue to be his confidante and the single most important influence on his intellectual and creative development through life.

On numerous occasions, Rilke held back the publication of the Christ *Visions*. The last time he did so was when his publisher, Anton Kippenberg of the Insel Verlag, asked for additional material to be included in a new volume of *First Poems* (*Erste Gedichte*). Rilke writes in a letter of January 8, 1912: I believe that "apart from the Visions of Christ, nothing usable will come of the search. And these great poems which I have not seen again for a long time, I must have about me for a while, and carry within my conscience, before they are to appear among people." The *Visions* appeared first in the third volume of *Collected Works* (*Sämtliche Werke*) in 1959 and in the hitherto only English translation of 1967. Rilke may have hesitated in having the *Visions* published for two reasons. First, they symbolized the beginning of his intimate relationship with Lou; and second, their depiction of Christ called into question orthodox church teachings, so that Rilke may have feared negative repercussions from a public not yet prepared to accept these views. Among these unorthodox views is the fact that the Trinitarian concept of God as Father, Son, and Holy Spirit is missing. The doctrine of Christ's death and resurrection is interpreted on a personal, individualistic level, not in the context of the church as Christ's body. And Christ is viewed as more human than divine and does not hold the exclusive position of mediator between God and humanity. Rather, Rilke's Christ is a unique, perennial teacher who by his human compassion, suffering, and solitude models a God search driven by feeling and an ethics of love. In his prophetic role, this Christ confronts people with their attachments and possessions and encourages them through self-surrender to imitate him and the behavior of the things of creation. Not by mere consent to Christian doctrine but by a complete surrender to God, by death to self, and through a childlike stance toward others and all of creation can people find themselves as if in union and harmony with all things and with God.

Besides *The Book of Hours* and *The Visions of Christ*, Rilke had written a third book of poems on a Christian theme. Titled *The Life of the Virgin Mary (Das Marienleben)*, this set of thirteen poems, published in 1912, describes scenes from the life of the Virgin Mary, based on the Gospel accounts and Christian legend. Initially drafted in 1900 while he was living at the artists' colony in Worpswede near Bremen, the poems were revisited by Rilke in 1912 and ten new ones written. The impetus for revisiting the Mary poems had come in 1911 from Heinrich Vogeler, a Jugendstil artist and founder of the Worpswede colony. Vogeler wanted to make drawings for the Mary poems and had approached Rilke's publisher about the possibility of their publication. After reviewing the old poems the publisher had sent him, Rilke retained two of them but wrote ten new ones. At the time, Rilke was staying at Duino, Italy, and its so-named castle, which was owned by the Austrian-born princess Marie of Thurn and Taxis-Hohelohe. It was also at this castle that only weeks after completing the Mary poems in the week of January 15 to 22, 1912, Rilke wrote the first two of the ten poems that would later be published in the collection *Duino Elegies (Duineser Elegien)*. Though the majority of these poems were written at Muzot, Switzerland, in 1922 and completed there, along with those in the volume *Sonnets to Orpheus* (*Die Sonette an Orpheus*), both published in 1923, Rilke retained the name of the place where the first two had emerged. While composing the Mary poems at Duino, Rilke had recognized the resurgence of a newly flowing creativity. When sending the poems off for publication in 1912, he described them in his note to Katharina Kippenberg, the wife of Anton Kippenberg, Rilke's publisher, as "the small mill of the Life of the Virgin Mary" that had been spun about by the underlying torrent of the *Elegies*. Rilke's visual inspiration for the cycle had been the church art of Italy, the Greek handbook of the monks of Mount Athos, and a Russian manual on iconography. In a letter to Countess Sizzo of June 1, 1922, Rilke admits to his indebtedness. Apart from the pictures of Italians, such as Titian or Tintoretto, "I am vastly indebted to and have been inspired by the famous recipe book of all paintings of saints, *The Painter's Handbook of Mount Athos* [1855], and even the so-called Kiewski Paterik [an orthodox Russian collection of suggestions and instructions for the depiction of biblical objects]."

✦

The thematic collection *On God* contains two letters by Rilke, the first an actual letter written during World War I on November 8, 1915, in Munich, the second a fictional one composed after the war, between February 12 and 15, 1922, in Muzot, Switzerland. The first letter was addressed to Lotte Hepner, who had read Rilke's novel *The Notebooks of Malte Laurids Brigge* (*Die Aufzeichnungen des Malte Laurids Brigge,* published in 1910) and was presumably grappling with the questions of suffering, the meaning of life, and the place of God in the world that the novel raises. The questions are presumed since we do not know her background nor have her letter, only Rilke's reply.

Rilke presents a view of God that builds on the one presented in *The Book of Hours:* again God is hidden and mysterious, and people are likely to discount and ignore God or to bracket him out of their life, thereby constructing a sanitized, arid version of life. Now, however, God is no longer the "neighbor God" who resides next door and begs to be drawn close. Rather, God is the one already residing in the person's heart and is fully present. The former fear that God may be weak, spent, and worn is unwarranted. For God is the essence of life, and God's apparent distance from us diminishes to the degree that we become open to life's questions, to the presence and reality of love and death, in short, to life itself. Both we and God, says Rilke, are facing in the same direction and are surrounded and infused by divine currents as by a great mystery. Our main task is to surrender to this mystery and especially to the reality of death, rather than resisting, ignoring, or hiding from it. Embellishing or displacing death into another life or into the world beyond prevents people from fully experiencing God in the here and now.

The second letter builds on this view of God as mystery that infuses every aspect of the visible world and human life. This fictitious letter in the persona of a factory worker addressing a poet was written while Rilke was working on the *Duino Elegies* and after he had completed the *Sonnets to Orpheus* in a mere three days, between February 2 and 5, 1922. It is also the last longer prose piece he wrote before his death. Rilke's factory worker labors mainly in the office, only sometimes at the machine, and his previous studies have equipped him for employing sophisticated language and thought in the letter. With the worker writing to a poet, "V."—who apparently is the Belgian poet Emile Verhaeren—Rilke had created for himself what Rüdiger Görner calls "his ideal reader and, more precisely, the ideal reader of the *Elegies* and *Sonnets* he just now had finished." The letter writer asks questions of the poet, describes critical life-changing experiences, and reflects on life's meaning. The letter's theme is a discussion of the nature of faith (though the word is not mentioned per se), of God, and of Christ. Most especially, it is a critique of the otherworldly orientation of Christianity, which has given Christians license to exploit and abuse the earth to their advantage. This otherworldly orientation has also emphasized Christ's personal suffering on the cross so that people have missed recognizing Christ's role as symbol and pointer to God's presence and power within them. They have resisted that power as it makes itself felt even in its unjust, arbitrary, and ugly forms by placing it outside themselves and failing to surrender to it and receive it. Rilke has the worker say that it is of little use to seek God in the Jesus of two thousand years ago, because he lived then and we live now. Jesus's role was to be index finger and role model in people's God quest. Unfortunately, people have tended to crowd around the cross and failed to look in the direction to which the crossbars are pointing; namely, God. By unreservedly receiving and accepting life's suffering, the heaviness within, and the concrete experience of life and death and joy and sorrow, symbolized by the cross and Christ's suffering on it, we are directing our gaze toward God and begin maturing as on a tree whose ripe "fruit" we are and whose maturity will be to God's benefit.

In the letter of the young worker, Rilke also criticizes the church's moralistic and life-negating stance in regard to the body, sexuality, and the experience of the sexual encounter. By denigrating or ignoring this side of human life, the church had failed to assist people in the one experience that most concretely and intimately allowed humans to feel close to God and to life's mystery. Since the church had shied away from addressing the physical reality of sexuality, people were left to behave like burglars, having to break into a forbidden enclosure at night and, like the semiconscious and half-dead, could experience only part of life without shame; hence, they were being derailed in their God quest and were missing out on life and God altogether. As with *The Visions of Christ,* Rilke did not publish the fictitious letter of a worker during his lifetime: After all, it was highly critical of the church, the church's representatives, and church teachings on the body and the person of Christ. For Rilke, a true teacher of God and interpreter of life's meaning was to be found not within the church but elsewhere. The true teacher took seriously the concreteness of this world, creation, the human body, human sorrows and pain, responsibilities and tasks, and human experience. Also, the true teacher refused to escape the world of the here and now and did not suggest a precipitous run toward a heavenly Jerusalem, for example, or declare people sinners in need of ecclesiastical mediators and "letter" writers. A true teacher on God did not offer doctrines on the afterlife that were little more than a spurious solace for one's unfulfilled, half-lived life on earth; rather, he or she offered ways for living concretely and fully in the world while seeking the transcendent God. For Rilke, such a true teacher is the poet.

I

Munich
Nov. 8, 1915

In so many ways, L.H.,[1] one could respond to your letter. Nearly each sentence of yours demands ten letters in reply. Not that one would have the answer to everything that is a question in it (and what in it is not a question?). But what you write are questions that have been repeatedly covered up by other questions or by what appeared to be more transparent under the influence of clearer questions, like a whole question dynasty. And who has ever answered them?

What is addressed in Malte Laurids Brigge,[2] and what is endured there (and please forgive me for bringing up this book again given that it brought us together), is actually the very thing that is the subject here, considered from every angle, again and again, and in every respect: How is it possible to live life when its elements are totally incomprehensible to us? We are always insufficient in giving love, uncertain in making decisions, and powerless regarding death. How then can one truly live? I wrote the book with the deepest internal obligation to address these questions and wanted to write about my amazement over the fact that for millennia now people have been dealing with life and death, even with God, hence with these first, most immediate, and—strictly speaking—only tasks: for what else is there for us to do and who knows for how long we will have to be facing them in our helplessness, like beginners, standing between terror and excuse like the poor. Is this not incomprehensible? Whenever I allow myself to become aware of my surprise over this fact, I am forced into the greatest despair and later on into a sense of dread. But even beyond such dread lies something and then something beyond that, which has such great intensity that my intuition is unable to determine whether it is burning hot or ice-cold.

Years ago I tried to answer someone who had been frightened by the Malte book by saying that I, too, considered it at times like a hollow mold, like a photographic negative, whose furrows and indentations are pain, sadness, and painful acknowledgment; but that the cast of the mold, provided one could produce it (as with a bronze, the positive figure one makes from the cast), might perhaps be happiness, affirmation, the most concrete and secure blessedness. Who knows, I wonder, if we are not always entering life as if from behind the gods' backs, separated from their radiant faces by nothing else than their own bodies, from their expressions that we so long for, to which we are so close and yet behind which we are standing. But that can only mean that our faces and the face of God are looking in the same direction, are in agreement with each other. And so, how should we ourselves then face the space that lies before God?

Am I confusing you by using the word "God" and "gods" (just as with the word "spirit" or "spirits") for the sake of inclusiveness and under the assumption that you, too, might be able to make immediate associations? Please try to accept the supernatural. Let us agree that since their earliest beginnings people have formed gods who here and there contained only what was dead and threatening, what was destructive and terrorizing, what was violence, anger, supernatural stupor, as if all equally strung together into a dense and evil knot. In short, one acknowledged the strange, if you will, saying one was aware of it, endured it, and even recognized a certain mysterious kinship and association with it: one was part of it, but did not know how to deal with these experiential facets of life. They were too big, too dangerous, too complex, and they grew far beyond oneself and assumed immense importance. Apart from the many challenges of an existence geared toward utility and performance, it was impossible to carry steadily along these other circumstances too, cumbersome and incomprehensible as they were. Hence, it was agreed to occasionally bracket them out. After all, they were an extra, the most powerful, the too powerful, the enormous, the forceful, the incomprehensible, the often ominous. And when thus gathered into one place, why would and should they not make themselves felt in their influence, effect, power, superiority? But now as if from outside ourselves. Could one not see the history of God like that: as if it were that side of the human condition that was never visited, always put off, saved up for later, and eventually missed out on altogether, a side that had demanded its own time, its own decision and determination; but now that it had been exiled to another place, it produced such tension that the individual heart, continually distracted and stingily applied, could hardly withstand it?

You see, that is how it was with death also. Death is experienced and yet we are not experiencing it in its true nature, ever growing taller than we are and yet never quite acknowledged by us, injuring the meaning of life and yet surpassing it from the start. Therefore, death too was exiled, pushed outside, so it would not constantly interrupt us as we were looking for life's meaning, this death that is most likely so close to us that we are incapable of measuring its distance from our very own soul. Death became something external that was to be kept at bay daily; it lurked somewhere out there in empty space so as to attack one or the other person in a malicious, haphazard way. Suspicion mounted against death for being the adversary of all adversaries, the invisible opposite out there in space, the one who brings our joys to an end, the dangerous glass of our happiness out of which we could be spilled at any moment.

Both God and death were now outside, were the other, while inside was our life, which at the cost of such an exclusion began to look human, familiar, possible, manageable, completely our own. But since this newly established and so-called beginner's version of life, this preliminary course, did not integrate and teach a great many things and did not allow one to strictly distinguish between the problems solved and those temporarily skipped, one made even in this shortened version no straightforward and reliable progress; instead, one ended up living from sum totals of which some were true, others false. Based on the end result, one had to recognize that the main mistake had been the presupposition that served as the foundation for this tentative construct of existence. By subtracting God and death from any applied interpretation of life's meaning, by regarding them as being not of this world, coming later, residing elsewhere, being different, one had accelerated the smaller cycle of the here and now. What is called progress became the happening of a self-enclosed world which had forgotten that, already from the start, it stood surpassed by death and by God, no matter how hard it tried.

If one had been able to relegate God and death to the province of mere ideas and mind constructs, a type of meditation could have been the result. But nature knew nothing of the repression we had somehow managed to achieve. When a tree begins to bud, both death and life spring up in it. The field is full of death, pushing away the rich expression of life by its fallow face, and the animals walk patiently from one to the other. All around us, death is still at home, and from between the cracks of things it observes us, and a rusty nail, somewhere protruding from a board, does nothing but look forward to death day and night.

Even love, which mixes up the numbers among people so as to introduce a game of proximities and distances where we always act as if the universe were full and no other room left but in us, even love does not respect our divisions, but pulls us, trembling ones, into a never-ending awareness of the whole. For lovers do not subsist on the segregated this-worldly life. Rather, they appropriate the entire immense wealth of their hearts as if no separation had ever been made. One can say about them that God becomes food for them and that death does not harm them: for they are full of death by being full of life.

But we must not *talk* about experience here, for that is a mystery, neither one closed off against the world nor one that demands to be hidden away. Rather, it is a mystery that is secure in itself, is wide open like a temple, whose doors take pride in being an entrance and whose columns are singing about being a portal.

In returning to your letter, one will have to ask how to do it, preparing ourselves for the experience that one day will meet us in human relationships, at work, through suffering, an experience for which we cannot be only vaguely prepared because the experience itself is very precise, so much so that it may meet us head-on, never as an accident. You yourself have discovered several paths of learning, and one can see that you have walked them attentively and thoughtfully. Consequently the shake-ups you mention did solidify you, rather than burying you. As far as I can, I should like to support your thinking about death, both its biological side (by referring you to Wilhelm Fliess[3] and his rather remarkable research: I will be glad to send you a little Fliess book in the next few days) and by referring you to some remarkable people who have thought about death in a rather pure, quiet, and exceptional way. To begin with there is Tolstoy.[4]

There is a story by him called "The Death of Ivan Ilyich." On the evening that I received your letter, I felt the strong urge to reread these extraordinary pages. And so I did and, while thinking of you, I almost read to you these lines out loud. This story is contained in the seventh volume of Tolstoy's collected works, published by Eugen Diederichs, along with "Walk While It Is Light" and "Lord and Servant." Do you have access to this book? I hope you have access to much of his work, such as the two volumes on "Stages of Life," "Cossacks," "Polikuschka," "Linen Measurer," and "Three Deaths." His enormous ability to experience nature (I hardly know another person who was so passionately connected with nature) enabled him to an amazing degree to think and write from the perspective of the whole, from an experience of life that was so permeated by a most evenly distributed death that it appeared to be contained in everything, as a unique spice added to the strong taste of life. And precisely because of it, this man could become so deeply and utterly frightened upon realizing that somewhere there was this pure death, the bottle containing death or this ugly cup with its broken handle and meaningless inscription "Faith, hope, love," from which someone was forced to drink the bitterness of undiluted death. Since being an observer of his own fear was natural to him, he observed in himself and others many forms of deathly fear. Hence, his relationship with death must have been a magnificently matured fear all the way to the end, a connecting link, an immense construct, a tower of fear with hallways and stairways and ledges without railing and with precipices on all sides. Only that possibly at the last minute, this strength by which he experienced and admitted to the effort such fear took, transformed into distant reality and suddenly became this tower's safe flooring to him, a landscape and heaven, and the wind and flying birds.

II

If I were a young worker, I would have written you perhaps the following:

At a gathering last Thursday, someone read to us from your poetry, Mr. V.,[5] and it affected me, so that I know no other way than to write to you about what I am thinking, as much as I am able to do so.

The day after said reading I accidentally attended a Christian gathering, and perhaps this was the true reason for the emotional spark, so that I am now headed in its direction with all my might. It takes enormous force to start something. I cannot start. I always skip over what should be the start. Nothing is as strong as silence. If we had not been born into the midst of speech, the silence would never have been broken.

Mr. V., I am not talking about the evening that your verses were read. I am talking about the other one. I feel compelled to say: who, well, I cannot express it any differently, who is this Christ that is meddling in everything? He did not know anything about us, about our work, about our misery, about our joy and the ways in which we work, suffer, and summon joy, yet who seemingly and persistently demands of us to make him first in our life. Or is this only being put in his mouth? What does he want from us? He wants to help us, one says. Yes, but he certainly acts rather helpless when around us. The conditions of his time were so very different from ours. Or is it not really a matter of historical conditions, so that if he entered my room here or the factory there, would then everything be alright? Would my heart make a leap and continue beating in a different shift, so to speak, always headed toward him? My feeling tells me that he cannot come, that it would make no sense. Not only are the externals of this world different, but the world has no door that would allow him access. He could not shine through a store-bought jacket; certainly, he would not shine through it. It is no accident that he walked about in a robe that had no seams, and I believe that the core of light in him, that which made him look so strong day and night, has long dissolved and been differently allocated. But I think given how great he was, one could have expected of him no less; namely, that he would somehow dissolve without any residue, without any kind of trace, undetectable.

I cannot believe that the cross was meant to remain; rather, it was to mark the crossroads. It certainly was not meant to be something to brand us everywhere. It should have dissolved in him. Is it not something like this: he wanted to simply create a taller tree on which we could more easily mature. He on the cross is this new tree in God, and we were to be warm, happy fruit at its top.

One should not always talk about the previous but should start with what comes afterward. It seems to me that this tree should become one with us or we with it and through it, so we need no longer concern ourselves with it but solely with God by remaining in him more purely and doing what Christ's ultimate intent was.

When I say the word "God," I do so with great conviction and not by rote. It seems to me that people use this word without thought, even if doing so from deep pensiveness. It may be well and good if this Christ should have helped us say the word in a firmer, fuller, more convinced tone of voice; but let us put a stop to involving him all the time. Let us not always feel forced to return to the hardship and sorrow he had to endure to "save" us, as you would call it. Let us finally start living this salvation. Otherwise the Old Testament would be at an advantage since, no matter where one reads in it, it is full of index fingers pointing to God, and one always finds someone who, upon growing heavy, falls straight into God. And once when I tried reading the Koran, I understood, in spite of my not getting very far into it, that there again is a powerful index finger and God stands where it is pointing to, ever in the process of his eternal rising in the east, which is never depleted. Surely Christ wanted the same. But people here were like dogs that do not comprehend the meaning of an index finger and think they have to snap at the hand. Instead of walking out into the night of sacrifice on the crossroads where now the signpost of the cross had been erected, instead of continuing to walk along this pathway of the cross, Christians have settled beneath it and have insisted that they are living there in Christ, even though in him there was no room, not even for his mother and not for Mary Magdalene, just as there is no room in anybody else who is merely pointing, who is gesture and not a place in which to settle.

For this reason, they do not really live in Christ, these people whose hearts are so stubborn and who are always reproducing him and are drawing their existence from erecting these crooked or completely windblown crosses. They will have to answer for the crowdedness there, this waiting around in a crowded place; they bear the guilt for the fact that the journey has not proceeded in the direction to which the crossbars are pointing. They have turned the Christian faith into a trade, a middle-class occupation, *sur place,* into a pond that alternates between being drained and being filled up again. Everything they themselves do according to their irrepressible nature, provided there is still some life left in them, stands in contrast to this construct of theirs, so that they continually muddy their own waters and then repeatedly have to renew them. Out of zeal, they never stop denigrating and devaluing what is of this world and which, after all, should fill us with joy and confidence. As a result, they increasingly hand over the earth to those who are ready to take from the one considered defective and suspect and seemingly unfit for anything else, what gives them at least a temporal, quick advantage. Does this increasing exploitation of nature not result from the fact that over the course of centuries the things of this world have been repeatedly devalued? What insanity to seek diversion with what is otherworldly when in this world we are surrounded by tasks and expectations and responsibilities for the future! What deceit to steal the delightful images of this world in order to sell them covertly as those of heavenly bliss!

It is high time that the impoverished earth should recall all that has been absconded from its happy state so as to refurbish its future. Does death really become more transparent with the abducted sources of light one has placed behind it? And since it is impossible that empty space can sustain itself, has not everything that was carried out of this world been replaced by a fraud? Is this the reason that the cities are filled with ugly artificial light and noise because one has exported true splendor with a song about a future Jerusalem to which one intends to move? Christ may have been right when speaking ill of earthly things in an age filled with stale and lifeless gods, even though I cannot help thinking that it borders on hurting God when our senses cannot perceive the perfect, utmost delight in what has been granted and offered to us, provided we are using it with the utmost care. The proper usage, that is it. To take in hand the earthly with a sense of wonder and in a heartfelt, loving way as all we have for the moment: that, to put it plainly, is God's great manual of operations, which Saint Francis of Assisi intended to record with his song to the sun, which at the hour of death seemed lovelier to him than the cross that, after all, just stood there pointing to the sun. By then, however, what one called the church had already grown into such an avalanche of voices that the song of the dying one was completely drowned out, except for being caught by a few simple monks and eternally affirmed by the scenery of its graceful valley.[6] How often have there been similar attempts at reconciling the Christian denouncement of the earth and its eye-catching friendship and serenity! Even elsewhere, even within the church and in its own crown did the things of the world forcefully reclaim their place in their innate abundance. Why does no one praise the fact that the church was strong enough to withstand collapse under the live weight of certain popes, whose throne was weighed down by illegitimate children, mistresses, and victims of murder? Was there not more Christianity in them than in the lightweight restorers of the Gospels; namely, something alive, unstoppable, transformed? After all, we have no concrete idea what the great teachings are supposed to become one day; one only has to allow them to flow and take their course and not frighten them off when they suddenly break through life's crevices and swirl around in unknown beds below the earth.

I once worked for a few months in Marseille. It was a unique time for me and I owe much to it. As it so happened, I met a young painter, who remained my friend until he died. He was suffering from a lung disease and had just returned from Tunis. We spent a lot of time together, and since the end of my assignment coincided with his return to Paris, we were able to spend a few days in Avignon. The days have remained unforgettable to me. The reason is in part the city itself, its buildings and surrounding areas, and in part because during these days my friend talked to me without pause and in a somewhat intense way about many things, especially his interior life, and he did so with the kind of eloquence that occasionally seems characteristic of people who are ill. Everything he said had a strange, powerful ring of truth to it. In everything that bubbled up and cascaded down during the almost breathless talks, one could see all the way down to the ground, the stones beneath the water. By that I mean to say that it was more than this world of ours here, was nature itself, was what is oldest and most solid in it, what we touch in so many places and on which we probably depend in the most pressing moments so that its current determines our decision. To that came an unexpected and happy experience of love he had had. For days, his heart was held up uncommonly high, which meant that the other side of his life had a spraying fountain shooting up to considerable heights. To see an extraordinary city and its more-than-pleasant surroundings with someone in such a disposition is a rare moment of grace. And so in looking back, these tender and passionate days of spring seemed to me to have been the only days of vacation I ever had in my life. To someone else, the time would have been so ridiculously short that it would have allowed for only a few impressions. But to me who was not used to having any free time, these days appeared vast. In fact, it seems almost incorrect to call it "time" when it was rather a new state of freedom, a quite tangible space, a being surrounded by a vast plain, and not something that passes. Back then I made up, so to speak, for a lost piece of childhood and early youth, for all that I never had the time to do. I looked, I learned, I understood. And from these days also stems the experience that makes it for me easy and true to say "God," so unproblematic and simple, as my friend would have said. How could I not see as enormous the house there that the popes had built for themselves? I was under the impression that it could not have an interior but had been built in solid layers of thick blocks, as if the exiled popes were interested only in demonstrating the weight of the papacy,[7] its prevalence, by piling it on the scales of history. And this ecclesiastical palace does in fact tower above an antique torso of a Hercules statue,[8] which is walled into its rocky foundations. "Did it not grow immensely," said Pierre about it, "as if from the kernel of a seed?"

That Christianity in one of its metamorphoses can look like that is much more comprehensible to me than trying to recognize its potency and taste in the ever weaker brew of tisane,[9] which is said to have been prepared from its earliest and most tender leaves. Even the cathedrals are not the body of the spirit that is being proposed to us as the essentially Christian one. I could see how among some of them might lie concealed the shaken statue of a Greek goddess:[10] so much growth, so much life had gathered in them, even though the fear born in them at the time had made them flee from this hidden body into the heavens, which were to be kept perpetually open by the sound of their big bells. Upon returning from Avignon, I frequently visited churches, in the evening and on Sundays, first by myself, and later . . .

I have a lover, who is almost a child still and who works from home, which during times of low production puts her in a difficult situation. She is skilled, could easily find a position at a factory, but she is afraid of the boss. Her idea of freedom is a life without bounds. You will not be surprised to hear that she perceives God, too, as a type of boss, indeed as the "arch boss," as she told me with a laugh and great terror in her eyes. It took her a long time to decide that she would come with me one evening to St. Eustache,[11] where I liked to go because of the music during the May masses. Once we even ended up at Maux[12] and looked at the tombstones in the church. Gradually she noticed that God does not bother people in church, that he does not demand anything; one might even think that he was not there at all, was he? As I was on the verge of saying so, Marthe[13] said that God is not there in the church, that there is something that prevents his presence. Perhaps it is what people themselves through the centuries have brought into this lofty, strangely fortified air. Perhaps it is because the silence of the powerful and sweet music can never completely escape to the outside and now has penetrated the stones; and they have to be strangely excited stones, these buttresses and arches. And even though a stone may be hard and penetrable only with great difficulty, it is still shaken again and again by the song and these attacks by the organ, these raids, these storms of song, each Sunday, like hurricanes on great festival days. The quiet before the storm is what actually is at work in these old churches. I told that to Marthe. The quiet before the storm. We listened, and she immediately understood, because she has such a wonderfully well-prepared nature. Since then, we have been going inside here and there when we heard singing, and we then stood there, close to each other.

The most beautiful moments for us were when we stood before a stained glass window, one of these old picture windows with many compartments, each completely filled with figures, big people and small turrets and all kinds of scenes. Nothing was too strange to be depicted. One sees there fortresses and battles and a hunting scene, and the beautiful white deer appears again and again in hot red and in blazing blue.[14] I once was given very old wine to drink. That is how they affect the eyes, these windows, only that the wine was a dark red in the mouth while these images here are also in the colors of blue and violet and green. There is really everything that can be found in these old churches, no reticence about it all, unlike the new ones, where only the so-called good examples appear. One finds here also what is painful and evil and terrible, that which is crippled, is in great need, is ugly—even injustice, and one would like to say that it, too, is loved for the sake of God. Here is the angel who does not exist and the devil who does not exist; and the human being who does exist is between both of them, and, come to think of it, the surreal presence of the first two makes the human being more real to me. I can do in there what I feel is called for: accept the person as a whole and do so more readily than on the street among people, who have nothing concrete about them. But it is difficult to express.

And what I now want to say is even more difficult to express. Namely, as far as the "patron" or power is concerned, there is only one means against it, something I also began realizing slowly while we were standing in there amid the music: to keep on walking in union with the power. Here is what I mean: one should try hard to see in any type of power that claims its right over us all the power there is, power as a whole, power at large, the power of God. One should say to oneself that there is only one power and perceive the small, the spurious, the defective power as if it were rightfully the one to make claims on us. Would it not be defused then? If one were always to see in any kind of power, even in the painful and malicious one, the one great power itself, I mean that which ultimately and justly retains its claim to it, would one then not survive unharmed, so to speak, even the power that is unjust and arbitrary? Do we not face all the other unknown great forces the same way? We experience none of them in their pure form. We first take any of them with all their defects that perhaps correspond to our own. When it comes to all the scholars, discoverers, and inventors, did not the mere assumption that they were dealing with great forces suddenly take them to the greatest of them all?

I am young and there is much rebelliousness in me. I cannot be certain that I will act in accordance with my insight in all situations, such as when impatience and dislike are sweeping me away. But deep down I know that submission goes further than resistance. It puts to shame that which overpowers, and it contributes greatly to the glorification of the one true power. The one who is resisted pushes beyond the center of power and perhaps is able to leave it; but beyond that he or she stands in an empty field and will now feel the need to search for another gravitational force to which to attach. And this next force may end up being even more arbitrary than the first. So, why not recognize in the power we first encounter the greatest force, undeterred by its weaknesses and vacillations? At one point, lawlessness will meet with law, and we will have saved our energies by leaving it to deal with itself and so be converted. Of course, this is part of the long and drawn-out processes that are in radical opposition to the strangely precipitous pace of our time. But besides the quickest movements, there will always be the slow ones, even those of such extreme slowness that we will no longer be able to witness their progress. Of course, this is the reason that humanity exists, is it not, so it can wait and see what reaches beyond the single individual. From humanity's perspective, the slow is often the fastest, which is to say that it turns out that we only called it slow because it was incomprehensible.

It seems to me that there exists something totally incomprehensible, which people never tire of mishandling by applying to it standards, measurements, and institutions. Especially when it comes to this love that they call "sensual" with an unbearable mixture of disdain, craving, and curiosity, one can see there the worst effects of this degradation that Christianity thought it had to bestow on earthly things. Here everything is distortion and repression, even though we ourselves are born from this deepest happening and we ourselves find in it the center of our delights. If I may say so, it is to me more and more incomprehensible how a teaching that calls us unjust precisely in the point where the entire creature enjoys its most blessed right is for the most part allowed with such consistency to prevail, even though it proves itself nowhere.

Again I am reminded of the animated talks I was permitted to have with my late friend, back then in the spring among the meadows of the Barthelasse Island,[15] and later. Yes, during the night that preceded his death (he died the following afternoon shortly after five o'clock), he offered me in a moment of utter suffering such pure sights that my life seemed to begin anew in a thousand different places, and when trying to reply I found that my voice had become unavailable to me. I did not know that there were tears of joy. I cried my first ones amateur-like into the hands of the one who would be dead the next day, and I felt how in Pierre the flood of life rose up once more and overflowed as these hot drops were added to them. Am I extravagant? After all, I am talking about a surplus here.

I am asking you, H.V., why is it that if one truly wants to help us, us who are helpless, why are we being deserted in that very place that is at the root of all experience? The one able to assist us there could be assured that we would not be asking him or her for anything else. For the assistance given then would grow by itself in our life and would become greater and stronger along with it. And it would never cease. All the things that get implanted into our innermost being! How we have to secretly circle it and finally we manage to penetrate like burglars and thieves, into our own beautiful sensuality, where we err about and hurt ourselves and stumble only to run back out into the twilight of Christianity like those who have been caught. If guilt and penance had to be invented for the sake of the inner tension of one's conscience, why did one not attach them to another body part, why did one drop them there and then wait for them to dissolve in our pure well, thus poisoning and muddying it? Why did sensuality have to become homeless for us, instead of allowing it to be the festive place of our responsibility?

I will gladly admit that it should not belong to us since we are not capable of being responsible for and managing such unlimited blessedness. But why can we not belong to God in this part, too?

A church person might point out to me that there is marriage, even though he or she is not unaware how matters stand with this institution. Also, it is of little use to move the desire to procreate under the light of grace; my sensuality is not just aimed at my progeny, but it is the mystery of my own life. And only because it is apparently not allowed to take a central place there, so many people have pushed it to the outer rim and hence lost their balance over it. What to do about it! The terrible untruth and uncertainty of our time has its cause in the fact that one has not admitted to the happiness of our sensuality, remains in this oddly crooked sense of guilt, which is increasing steadily and which separates us from the rest of nature, even from the child. However, the child's innocence, as I came to find out in the course of this unforgettable night, does not consist in not being aware of its own sensuality, but, as Pierre said almost tonelessly, this incomprehensible happiness that wakes in us in one place in the middle of a close embrace still lies in the child's body equally distributed throughout and without name. To describe the strange location of our sensuality, one should have to say: at one time, we all were child, now we are child only in one place. But if only one person among us could truly understand this and had the ability to produce evidence for it, why then are we allowing for the fact that one generation after another finds itself under the debris of Christian prejudice and makes motions there in the dark like someone half-dead and is in the tightest grip of all these denials!?

Mr. V., I keep writing and writing. Almost an entire night has gone by. I will have to summarize. Did I tell you that I work in a factory? I work in the office, and sometimes I also work on a machine. A while back I was able to study for a short period of time. Well, I only want to say how I feel. You see, I want to be useful to God the same way I am here by what I do. I want to do work that is aimed at him without having my inner glow dimmed, if I may call it that, and not even by Christ, who once was water to many. The machine, for example, I cannot explain it to him because he does not recall it. I know that you are not laughing at me when I say so naively that this is for the best. With God, on the other hand, I have the feeling that I can take it to him, my machine and its first fruit and all my other work besides; he has no problem taking it all in. It is the same as it was once for the shepherds for whom it was easy to bring to the gods a lamb or the fruit of the field or the beautiful dove.

You see, Mr. V., I was able to write this long letter without even once having to use the word "faith." For that appears to be a complicated and difficult matter, and it is not for me to address it. I do not want to be called bad on account of Christ but want to be good for God. I do not want to be addressed beforehand as a sinner; perhaps I am not. I have such pure mornings! I could talk to God, and I need no one to help me write letters to him.

I know your poetry only through that reading the other evening. I own only very few books, which mostly relate to my work. Still, there are a few that deal with art and something on history, whatever it was I was able to get. The poems, however, and this you will have to allow me to tell you, have evoked this stirring in me. My friend once said: give us teachers who can praise what lies here in this world. You are one such teacher.

Letters to a Young Woman

monologue," as is somewhat typical of Rilke's letters, but contain some "moments where Rilke reveals his most radical interior to another person, even imposing it." Because Rilke forgoes playing the role of "ladies' man," "the basic questions of life move into clear focus," largely so also "because Lisa Heise not only sets the tone for that but also provides the theme." Though Rilke never met Heise in person, the exchange is personal: the poet listens and responds with the nuanced sensitivity of someone who seeks to understand and has no other motive than that of being present.

What can today's reader glean from the poet's responses? To Rilke fans, his letters to Heise offer fascinating detail about the last years of the poet's life, his frame of mind, the guiding themes of his thought, and the conditions under which he created his last two and perhaps greatest works, the *Elegies* and the *Sonnets*. But are there other insights also? As if anticipating the question, Carl Sieber, in his closing comments of the 1930 edition of *Letters to a Young Woman,* chronicles the various stages that occur when someone writes a letter to a well-known person, such as a poet. At the beginning, "there is a reaching out to the other through a letter that is mostly written to oneself." Then a relationship develops that is based on sympathy, mutuality, and understanding. And finally, "the poet's will to help offers help to the one seeking it." If what is offered "can exist apart from the specific human relationship, then it is not just helpful for the individual but also for others who are in similarly difficult situations." In these letters, readers will find in Rilke the sensitive and compassionate listener and the patient teacher on life who with equal degrees of detachment and receptivity can affirm and guide the movements of another person's soul, not unlike a spiritual director would today.

I think, dear Madam, that I cannot answer the lines you are writing me any better and more precisely than by assuring you that I understand your impulse from which they have sprung. The object of art cannot change anything or improve anything the way it is; it faces people in the same way that nature does, full in and of itself, occupied with itself (like a fountain), or, if one wants to call it that, indifferent. But we know that this second nature that is reticent and self-restrained is also made up of human elements, wrought by the extremes of suffering and joy, and therein lies the key to the treasure chest of unbounded solace, which appears to be gathered in the work of art and to which especially the solitary person can claim a special, an inexpressible right. I know that there are moments in life, years perhaps, where one's solitude in the midst of others reaches such a high degree that one would not have admitted to it if mentioned during times of casual, ordinary social gatherings. Nature cannot reach out to the person; rather, one has to have the strength to reinterpret it and woo it, translating it, so to speak, into human form in order to be able to draw near its smallest part. But this is precisely what one is unable to do when feeling absolutely lonely: one wants to be receiving a gift, unconditionally; one cannot afford to reach out, just as people at a low point of their vitality can barely open their mouths for the bite that is offered. That which really wants to reach us and is meant to do so has to come over us, as if it felt nostalgia for the person, as if it had no other purpose than to take over the other's life so as to transform every atom of life's weakness into surrender. Even then, strictly speaking, nothing has really changed. It would be presumptuous to expect a work of art to help one. An object of art contains the tension in human life without appropriating it, and its inherent intensity derived from mere presence can, without exaggeration, give the impression of ambition, demand, invitation, wooing and captivating love, stimulation, call: that is the worthy calling (not function) of the work of art. And this illusionary relationship between the work of art and the lonely person is like all those priestly illusions by which, since the beginning of time, the divine has been invoked.

I am immodestly explicit, but your letter has truly spoken to me—to me, not someone else who happens to have been addressed with my name by the letter writer—so that I wanted to be no less specific from my end and not offer you a platitude but rather the genuine, actual experience of being touched.

The fact that you talk about your child lends your letter a touch of trust, which I can return in no other way than by a most ready willingness to take on that trust. If it were to give you pleasure, please tell me about this child and about you, even if it were to entail many pages. I am among those people, those old-fashioned ones, who still consider the letter a means of conversation, one of the most beautiful and promising ones. Of course, I have to add now that this attitude occasionally multiplies my correspondence beyond what I can handle, that often for months the work, or rather (as was the case during the entire war) an insurmountable "secheresse d'Âme" [dryness of the soul] keeps me quiet and dumb. But then I do not gauge human relationships in parsimonious and ever calculating human terms, but along those of nature.

If you wish, may these lines then from now on serve as a connection and rendezvous between us. I will be absent for a long time, but, if you like, always be present again, knowing, understanding the way I was allowed to do today for the first time.

Rainer Maria Rilke

Soglio (Bergell, Graubünden), Switzerland
August 30, 1919

Dear Madam,

From the start I want to clarify: be assured that never will
one of your letters, as long as you choose to delight me with
this communication, be a burden that begs an immediate response. The experiences you express, the nature of your disposition that you allow me to see from afar are actually outside
the realm that would entail "responding" to them. These questions of yours constitute the inquiring nature of our innermost
self, and who could reply to it? Perhaps happiness, ill fortune,
an unexpected moment of the heart overcomes us suddenly
in the form of a response, or it takes place in us gradually and
inconspicuously, or a person opens it up for us, this response,
so that it overflows from the look that a person gives us and
makes for a fresh, previously unknown page of the heart we are
reading to the other. But allow this page to be read out loud;
did it not start with a question? Which human experience and
which expression of human nature does not eventually climb
up the small hill of the question and then stand there in open-
ness, but open to what? Open to heaven.

The nature of a woman: it wants to be fulfilled, acted upon,
responded to, once and for all, because unanswered questions
are against her nature. But do not forget that the man stands
facing this nature of the woman, just as each one of us is facing nature: incapable, that is, of comprehending the inex-

haustible wealth, receiving, breathing in and letting go again, looking away from nature, losing ourselves in the cities, falling away from nature and into the intervals of existence through books, negating and denying it in each of the habits of sleeping and being awake, until a wave of discontentment, the ruins of disappointment and weariness, a concrete pain pull us back to nature's heart, casting us down before nature which always *is*, throwing us, the ones who were on the verge of dying. Yet nature, which is complete and ever active and at rest, does not notice when we depart from it. Independent of our heart's passion or departure, nature always has us with it, not knowing the plight of loneliness; or perhaps nature is solitary in its completeness because it is everything and no longer lives on the boundaries but in the warm, complete middle and center. Should not woman, the lonely one, have the same place of refuge in herself, in the concentric circles of her own nature, which ever returns to her whole? As far as woman is nature, she can perhaps manage to do so at times, but then her contradictory basic disposition takes revenge on her, so that she is forced to be both nature and human being wrapped into one, the inexhaustible and the exhausted. And out of exhaustion and not from a sense of voluntary surrender, from the fact that she is not allowed to continue giving and going, her own proffered wealth becomes a burden in her well-stocked heart since the high and happy demand is missing to which she is supposed to wake up in the morning and which she is able to meet even without words and while quietly asleep. Yes, then her nature is in a state where in her own earthy wealth the flowers no longer want to raise their heads and grow, of a disposition from which the young rabbits would be fleeing and the birds would be flying away without falling back into their welcoming nests. But if she wants to be true to her nature and recognize her right to be caring, giving, and nurturing beyond measure, she will not continue to remain confused by her human mind.

She will not ask whether the protection she is offering is really reliable, whether giving truly knows no limits, whether perhaps there lurks a cunning strategy that only wants to receive, a strategy that nature does not know. Is a woman's nature not largely at risk and unsecured? How dare she make promises when at any moment she, the human being, can experience the dearth of her heart, a consuming misery, an illness that spoils the sweetness of her breath and turns the gleam in her eye into twilight?

I, too, have often imagined that the dual nature of woman should be made more bearable through the pure love offered to her by the man; but at most he only participates in the reality and love of his beloved without making good on the promise of love. As a suitor, he exaggerates the forces of nature to the awed girl, only to be the first shortly after his conquest to deny her and to complain about the human weakness and helplessness of the one creature that even now completely surpasses him. Herein can be seen the abject passivity of a man's love, which had only enough breath for a festival day and enough resolve for the immeasurable gift of one night. And no, his love was not vibrant enough to make use of it for himself and to transform it completely, to create for it the silence that restores the indispensable innocence between lovers and without which they will be unable to remain together. Thereby, and in contrast to the woman, the man seems to be in the wrong, a braggart in matters of love who makes no progress beyond the beginners' stage on the subject, continuing to think that by rehearsing the poem's first lines he has recited it in its entirety. All the while, the woman shows him in image and rhythm how to do it correctly. Does not the man end up then on the other side, as someone to be pitied in his dilemma of passing by, having passed by, being the blind, the precipitous one who wants to travel around the world and is not capable of completing one full circle around a heart?

This, then, about one of your evenings. It is strange: perhaps it is especially the evenings of "unbearable depths" that people like you and me long for, provided they do not misjudge their danger; for these in particular should be the most challenging to one's interior, demanding the most of the heart because they have ultimately no other ending but a new birth. For a long time now my outer and inner circumstances have not allowed me to have such evenings. What a blessing this quiet, beautiful, old house of yours seems to be. And how comforted I feel momentarily in my homelessness when you say that a single letter of mine was able to meet the expectations of your festively opened room!

Rainer Maria Rilke

This, dear Madam, hardly will turn into a letter but can only be a caring inquiry about you. Your letter of September 28 concluded with the indication of many uncertainties and changes, so that I was inclined to attribute the long pause to all kinds of difficulties. It would be good if you could assure me somehow.

In regard to my own silence, I kindly asked of you from the start to never conclude from it a lack of interest or my forgetting you. I have long periods of stagnation where I loathe the fountain pen and am in other respects, too, very much influenced by changes and conditions in my surroundings, so that I could not vouch for any kind of consistency. If I ever were to find the right and agreeable spot where everything conducive to work and concentration could blend, and I infinitely long for such a place, I would certainly improve in this regard and would become more productive and reliable. As it appears, I am still far from it. The fatal, often bottomless makeshift arrangements into which the war has forced us are, by the looks of it, not bound to come to an end anytime soon, and I am ever *sur la branche, et c'est une branche plutôt sèche et très peu convenable qui me soutient* [on a branch, and this branch is rather dry and not quite fit to support me]. Just now when your last letter arrived, I had to give up my place of refuge in Soglio,[1] and with that began the unstable hotel life,[2] which remains so unprofitable when it comes to correspondence, in part because the hotels, even the so-called best ones, are never offering an appropriate writing spot, only perhaps to traveling government officials; in part because each time I am surrounded by so many personal and verbal exchanges, all my energies end up being drained by them. In addition, I was involved for five weeks in a type of touring engagement,[3] which for purposes of public readings took me from city to city and which created conditions, as you can well imagine, that increased as a matter of course the intensity of immediate personal exchanges. I am telling you all this not in order to weigh you down with my affairs—in fact, please forget about them as quickly as possible—but as a small attempt at an apology. After all, I am bound to assume that hearing from me would have been especially welcome for you during these unstable days. But perhaps these weeks were so full of activity, of decision and action for you that a letter would hardly have made a difference. Where did you find a place to live with your little son? I often wondered about it, and especially around Christmastime I thought about it a lot. Back then, you wrote about female students without indicating, however, the subject you teach. Were you able to resume teaching at your new place and successfully so, even perhaps with joy? What sacrifice it must have been for you having to leave the old, quiet house; I could empathize with you since I am someone without a homeland or a home. How different even these terrible war years would have been for me if only I had lived under the protection of consistent and affirming things.[4]

The "questions" of your long letter—well, dear Madam, where does one start? It all is invariably a matter of the "whole," is it not? But this whole, even when once in a while we are able to summon it internally in a spurt of happiness or by a purer strength of will, this whole is, in reality, broken up by the errors, mistakes, incompetence, by the evil committed between one person and another, by the disconsolate and the muddy, by apparently almost anything that concerns us on a given day.

It is frightening to presume that the instance of love, which we consider completely and deeply and uniquely our own, could be governed also from beyond the individual, such as from the perspective of the future (the future child) or, conversely, from the perspective of the past. But even if this were the case, there would still remain the experience of its indescribable depth, which belongs to the individual. And I am inclined to believe that. It would match the experience where the incomparable nature of each of our deepest delights is detached from permanence and continuity, so that these delights stand upright on the lines of our life's direction, like death, too, stands upright. And these moments have more in common with death than with all the goals and movements of our vitality. Only from the perspective of death (provided one does not see it as what no longer exists but suspects in it an intensity that decidedly surpasses us), only from the perspective of death, I believe, can one do justice to love. But even then, the traditional understanding of both of these terms produces ongoing and distracting obstacles. Our traditions no longer provide guidance, are dry branches that no longer can absorb the nurturing substance of the root. And if one adds to that the distractedness, lack of concentration, and impatience of the man, along with the fact that the woman is only truly giving during the rare moments of deep happiness, and that next to these two separate and shaken people there is the child that comes next, surpassing both of them and yet being equally helpless; in light of all this, one has to humbly admit that we do not have it easy.

Let us continue all that is between us most cordially from one time to the next.

Rainer Maria Rilke

Castle Berg on Mount Irchel, Canton Zurich, Switzerland
March 7, 1921

If small details can sometimes mean more than big assurances, I should like to show my intense interest by the fact that shortly after your letter arrived,[5] I opened my address book and carefully entered your new address. I can assure you that I wrote the name beautifully, unwittingly, for how could one not experience all the way into one's hand the gladness that comes with knowing the place of a "completely fulfilled existence"?

At first I wanted to say that your beautiful letter was not easy to understand, but that would not be correct: it is only difficult to render this understanding, this having understood. For everything that you report based on your experience can be affirmed by you alone, and even the most careful affirmation by someone else would run the risk of pinpointing to some moment of an indescribably fluctuating situation and hence be disrupting the natural freedom you experience when taking stock of these new conditions in which you find yourself. By contrast, one can use many more words with the solitary person, for someone else's insights place proverbial borders on the solitary's spaciousness to which the person, being almost without bounds, could gain no relationship otherwise. But for someone who is experiencing happy changes, life is filled with realities; hence this person should be neither held back from making discoveries nor be prepared for the next one. The activity of this person is clearly the opposite of the solitary one;

it is centrifugal, and the gravitation that takes effect in him or her is unpredictable.

If my actual understanding expresses itself in fewer and less clear words, then at least I need not fear to be interrupting you when simply acknowledging the particular kind of joy you give me with every word about your new experiences. Something was bound to come along that would welcome you; but now that this fulfillment, so most generous and completely rich in itself, has happened, one can see that you deserved this experience and, moreover, its richest kind. In retrospect, I now wish I had practiced the same generosity toward you that now comes so easily for me, back when to your loneliness was added the heaviness of the break with everything familiar. It is rare that a person can make deep and serious self-discoveries during a period of happiness and fulfillment. Most people see the results of their previous solitude as the errors of gloom; they throw themselves into the illusions of happiness and forget and deny the contours of their inner reality. Your self-preparation, on the other hand, was more thorough since you did not give up any of your previous insights, and all the insights about your plight and solitude appear now in the big gleam of radiant receiving and the counterradiance of giving, right at the center. On account of that, your happiness receives pure validation, fortification, a deep assurance where you find something in yourself to be "indestructible"; in a determined and honest way, you brought with you into the new happy environment a dowry that many would have considered too serious.

Apart from this big joy, I also see several smaller ones accompanying your news. How Michael is now being compensated for the temporary loss of the old garden, and how rewarding it must be to both of you to try to catch up with this fast-paced season by your gardening activity!

As for me, I live all by myself in this old, small castle called Berg, with its park and its fountain in front of the quiet windows. This is finally the kind of solitude I had hoped for since I came to Switzerland in order to resume my work; this work, however, even in these most fortuitous surroundings, is long and slow!

Rainer Maria Rilke

This time, you have added to the normal heightened expectation of the Christmas season by something of yours, something
very dear: your letter reached me on Christmas Eve, and what
was most beautiful about it is that all of its contents were such
a complete fit for the unique, still hour and contributed to it
fully with all you had to report. Do you really know (I often
wonder now in retrospect) how much of these years of effort
and friendship will remain as what is best in human nature and
in this world, and do you sufficiently foresee what they will
come to mean, regardless of how life unfolds? You may well
believe it; it is much, it is the most that can happen to a person. This being bent over and being tied to another is a most
tangible kind of work, coupled with the steady proof of a loving, mutual, kindred friendship, and with the development
and growth of your child, who gives a most robust expression
of all this growth by the games he plays. And if this were not
enough to convince you, you should find the purity of your
attitude confirmed by the strength, grace, truthfulness of your
disposition: how you were allowed to experience the excess
of the city and right next to it the staid measure of the violin
and then subsequently the fullness of the sea—and all of that
like an angel would have done who momentarily was walking
through the world of humans. I say all of this so explicitly to
emphasize how much your letter did become a Christmas letter, for it is only with the gesture of reflecting your experience

back to you in a deep, intensified way that I can sufficiently express my gratitude for your beautiful, attentive gift. Do not call your gift something "too personal." Only a small step and it would again become the most general, the ultimately valid, the basis of life, the longing for its basic colors and finally for eternal light, where every single one is a never-ending surrender.

Your small pictures, too, do not make the letter "too personal." I was very delighted to be looked at by all of you, even by your many flowers, and I have held very still so that everything could truly meet me. This land that you wrestled with, did it not somehow become to you in its innocent, flowery resilient opposition like the struggle of Jacob!? When looking at these small pictures one is reminded of far distances in a still sparsely populated area. How does one find this in the relatively densely populated Weimar region? Now you are experiencing in daily life the nature of your former three elements: the sky, the tree, and the plowed ground, their closures and the power of their disclosures; but that you should also be allowed to experience the fourth dimension for the sake of the space within, namely, that of the sea, does this not create an almost masterful balance in life?

You see now, don't you, what joy, what strong participatory emotion your letter was able to stir up. And as my letter is making you aware of that, it may well belong in this small, somehow saved-up antechamber of a new year that invariably seems to emerge between Christmas and the change of the year's number. To look at the number in this way means making a wish, does it not? To press matters, I am allowing one of these red "tiny good-luck beetles" with black dots [ladybugs] to wander across the writing paper since they are hibernating a little dreamily in my study.

Should I say something about myself in closing? You note the different address. In May, I had to leave the good Berg, which had given me such friendly shelter for one winter; again

I was faced by complete uncertainty and a fearful heart since the work for which I had sequestered myself in Berg had progressed by only half a step. This means that my entire summer was spent in a helpless and very pressing preparation for the coming winter, the one that should offer again equally quiet, solitary, and sheltering conditions. But how to find them, especially since, as you say, the "world is in flames"? For some time it looked as if I had to leave Switzerland altogether, which would have intensified my sense of being without a homeland because beyond there the "whereto" would have loomed large with its ghostlike deceptions. Almost as if to provide me with the greatest farewell possible, I traveled to Wallis, this most extraordinary canton, and almost no longer Swiss, to judge by its name, which I had discovered a year earlier[6] and which could evoke in me at once the lost, open world: that is how much it reminded me of the Provence with its powerful and inexpressibly gracious landscape, even of certain formations in Spain.

Here, by the strangest of coincidences, I found a small estate, where no one had lived continually for centuries, and from then on it was a long struggle for and with this strong, old tower, which (not so long ago) ended with something that could be called victory since in it I actually have managed to remain and build a nest for the winter! It was no small thing to "domesticate" Muzot, and without the assistance of a Swiss friend,[7] the entire enterprise of occupying it would have failed again because of practical obstacles. You see, my habitation (of course I am completely alone with only the housekeeper here) is no bigger than yours. The small picture, however, does not show fully its condition today. The picture must have been taken prior to 1900. Around that time, the owner changed, and the old estate underwent a thorough renovation, which fortunately did not change much and ruined nothing; actually, only the increasing decay was halted. A small garden was added that obediently wraps around the rock structure and has established itself. My most beautiful surprise was to find inside a regional tile stove of 1656, beamed ceilings from the same period, and even very well made and beautifully seasoned tables, chests, and chairs, all of them showing in their wood carvings the praiseworthy dates of the seventeenth century.

Something like that would certainly mean much to someone who knows how to appreciate and convey the tradition of things, as I have been apt to do since childhood. But the most generous extras are the surrounding areas of the spacious Rhône valley with its hills, mountains, castles, chapels, its solitary, magnificent poplars, raised like exclamation points in just the right places, its graceful paths around the vineyards resembling the curve of silk ribbons: in short, one is reminded of pictures one saw as a child where, for the first time, one was struck by the vastness and the open space of the world and the joy of beholding it. How beautifully each would promenade before you, I think!

And with that I send you greetings.

Rainer Maria Rilke

Your beautiful, heartwarming letter, way back in April! But how far you underestimate its ability to speak to me when in closing you express the wish that I receive it "cordially"! To be closer to the truth, you should have used "joyfully." And this word would have had to be written in very large letters. What good things you have had to report; do you fully realize how good it is what you are telling me? At times, perhaps, you sense the clang of the pure, hard metal of reality, but I, from my end, can hear you honestly and fervently stirring, the sound, the sound of bells, and I experience its overall importance in its freedom and breath.

Your entire difficult and unrelenting winter in all its harshness[8] must have been a type of frozen gladness, a block of pure, strong future, which now has dissolved, I hope, into a flowing, rushing stream running into spring. Now our gardens are sending each other greetings! In mine I planted (though hardly by doing it myself since I lack practice, experience, and know-how), more than a hundred roses; my work with them is confined to watering them every evening. No great variation in that, only being equally fair to each is what matters, and yet, since in all things it is the nuance that counts, one can use even the quietly dispensed water to give modestly something of oneself and infuse it into the eternally receiving growth, provided one does so attentively and with thoughtful care.

What surprises and inspires me is your strong and skilled strength by which you diligently devote yourself to the land under the most difficult circumstances. I for my part lack the skill for it and the economy of action. If I try nonetheless, it is not without haste, and what is more contrary to gardening than haste, than rush? But to make the transition from mental work to manual labor, what joy and freshness this could be! How one could learn from the other and benefit, provided one had some measure of know-how, certainty, experience, firmness, or, in one word, aptitude. I will probably have to make do with gardening within myself and watch others, deeply observing, possibly the way I watch your flowers and letters (both of which are unfolding in equal faithfulness).

My internal gardening was magnificent this winter. The suddenly restored awareness of my deeply prepared ground provided me with a great season of the spirit and a long-lost radiant strength of the heart. The dearly beloved work, begun in 1912 in magnificent solitude and since 1914 almost completely interrupted, could be resumed and could be completed with never-ending ability. Along with it came a small work, almost unintentional, a tributary, more than fifty sonnets, called the sonnets to Orpheus and written as a requiem for a girl who died young.[9] (Seven of them I have copied into a small notebook, which I enclose here.) If the selection had been larger or if I could have shown you the large main work, you would notice how in some places the happenings of our winters are similar. You write about being fulfilled at any given moment, carrying a surplus within, a possession that at close look immediately outweighs and contradicts all later potential privations and losses. I have experienced precisely this during this long winter in the depths of my work, more intensely and more irrevocably than I had known before: that life has long preceded any later poverty by its most extravagant riches.

What then is there to fear? Only that one might forget about it! But around us, in us, so many aids for remembering.

Rainer Maria Rilke

Château de Muzot sur Sierre (Valais), Switzerland
February 2, 1923

The very fears and immense, frantic happenings that cause you so much suffering allow me to grow more and more quiet. How often did I decide and then delay answering your agitated letter sent before the last, hoping for a better and more opportune hour: I wanted you to fully know how your letter (with its big four-page leaf) was received by me, by my heart. But my summer and even more so the fall were haunted by many uncertainties, and when I try during this winter, solitary as I am in my old tower, to make it resemble more the good one preceding it, then even here are difficulties, in part because my health is unstable, in part on account of those persistent disruptions, which then report the general turn for the worse to everything one wants to start (just as was the case during the war!). In that regard, I can quite literally take as my own a sentence of yours, such as: "Already during the day half of my thoughts are no longer mine, and the nights are filled with feverish visions." That one and others. For I feel no different than you. What is happening? And what is our place in these happenings? Just like during the war, one is pulled persistently into what has nothing to do with us, into a foreign disaster in which one becomes implicated. Does it not often feel as if with one deep breath one could rise above it? Often also one chances upon some inconspicuous comforting thought in the soul, which immediately makes itself known as if out of previously restrained riches, like on a walk through summer meadows where one brushes against something flowering below and which responds by releasing its scent. Your letter is full of such surprises, full of these pure aromas of the heart that only someone who has walked through utter poverty can know.

The way I see it and experience it based on my background and personal nature, there is little doubt that it is Germany which, by not knowing itself, is obstructing the world. The diverse composition and varied training of my blood provide me with a strange, distant perspective that allows me to see it this way. In 1918 at the moment of collapse, Germany could have put to shame and shaken up everyone and the world by an act of utter honesty and repentance: by a visible, decisive renunciation of her falsely developed prosperity; in a word, by the kind of humility that would have been so innately her nature and her basic honor that would have preempted everything one wanted to dictate to her from the outside. Back then I had hoped, for a moment, that there could have been inserted and restored after the fact in the German countenance, now strangely one-sided and willful, the era's lost trait expressed in the humility that makes Dürer's drawings look so rich.[10] Perhaps there were a few people who could feel that, whose wishes and hopes were aimed at such a correction. But the fact that this did not happen can already be noticed, and it is taking its revenge. Something was omitted that could have restored the proper balance. Germany has neglected to regain her purest and best, a restored balance based on her oldest foundation. She did not regenerate in its core and change her mind, did not create the type of dignity that has at its root the deepest humility, instead was only out for salvation in a superficial, rash, dishonest, and greedy sense, wanted to succeed and climb up and escape, instead of doing what is her innermost nature, namely, enduring, overcoming, and anticipating her own miracle. She chose to be stubborn instead of being willing to change. And so one can feel it: something has been remiss. A date is missing which could have been a signpost. A rung on the ladder is missing, hence the indescribable worry, the fear, the "premonition of an abrupt and powerful fall." What to do? Let us each stay on our small island of life which still remains quiet and yet is reliable, doing there what is expected of us, bearing and experiencing what is ours. Mine is no more permanent and secure than yours: I am guest where you are tenant. But now your lease is to be cut short for sure in the fall, now that you have reawakened and developed the landlord's land during the past three years? Is there no possibility to convince him otherwise? I can imagine how infinitely difficult it must be to find another similar position at this time. Going to Argentina has little appeal to you and your desires, since you have connections with something more familiar, a place on earth that knows you somehow. Besides, even there conditions no longer are the way they used to be, conditions that would enhance one's courage and strength.

Still, what results there have been, what a full and vast harvest when one looks back over the years in Weimar! So certain is this profit that even if you had not drawn a line and subtly indicated the sum total of it on the third page of your letter, I still could have made out by reading in your lines as from a ledger, the good, healthy fullness, even in those filled with fear.

That allows me to continue ever hoping for your very good, which I wish for you and which you have become so deeply capable of appreciating.

RMR.

Château de Muzot sur Sierre (Valais), Switzerland
January 27, 1924

So we each have been observing with concern the silence of
the other! My first gesture was to turn the letter over, and when
I recognized the old address, I almost thought that part of my
worries had been unnecessary. But that was not the case. Yes,
your letter shows me how difficult it all has become for you.
I cannot immediately grasp that it is the way you are describing it, but that is not a lack of understanding on my part, for
I understand your feeling of helplessness, your weariness, the
deep and utter disappointment of your soul when you now,
after so much true achievement, are no longer surrounded by
it. More than I can say it, I had hoped with you that it would
pay off, this honest wrestling with the earth. Well, to be honest, I see that my hope is still there. Is it not possible to take a
moment for reflection? You are writing about rushed plans?
Were there not many others made besides, is there not one
that could still be considered, is there not something closer
besides this going to a faraway place? The frame of mind in
which you speak to me is not the kind that allows for making important decisions. I would suggest that you do anything
you can to postpone a decision. Even if it all were to have to
start all over again as if nothing had been accomplished, you
should definitely take a vacation, a respite, even if it were only
the smallest carefree break from all these troubles. And such
a new beginning on a new clod of earth: does it really have to

be in the New World, was there no other piece of land found that would allow you to continue work in Germany? But how tedious to ask this question from my end here since you assure me that is the way it is. Still, since you have used the word "rushed," how could a friend not remind you that at such turning points the rushed leads to harm. And how could he not intimately understand you when you say that you now deserve some "quiet and stability."

It appears that there are countries whose crowded conditions no longer permit external influences to be controlled. Again and again, each one of us discovers that what could have quite easily "worked out" and restored balance to one's interior in a less distraught world did not come to pass. Providence is lacking, that which normally responded to us when we reached the end of our efforts, the "play" is missing, the wonderfully innocent game of give-and-take of the circumstances that offered possibilities, turns, directions by the way we naturally met them from our end, the quiet responding from the depth of destiny which at other times occurred when a true question, one we often were unaware of, had grown up in us. I see currently a number of people who are in difficulty because their presumed wages did not come. Those who are driven by greed or desperation cannot marvel when their striving remains uninterrupted; they know nothing of an internal arriving. At this moment, I am completely sympathetic to you. I try to understand what you are going through, and it is not difficult for me to be present in your heart. But I am without counsel. I sense that injustice is happening to you, but ever since the war years, injustice has become oddly insistent, and there is no other refuge from it than in one's innermost being. And in this regard especially, you have become stronger, less vulnerable, and more secure through the work of these years. That you are presently unable to redeem that should not distract you. The weariness, the disappointment, the ongoing worry prevent you from having control of yourself, and thus it also seems as if you were leaving all that is familiar.

Would you believe that I was always held back from sending you the elegies;[11] I sensed your distractedness and that it would not be the right time to propose to you such an extensive and often difficult reading. At the same time, I was held back too by a repeated feeling of illness, which recently became so burdensome that I submitted to being observed by a doctor, just like last summer, from which I was released only last week. For the past twenty-three years and in so many countries and circumstances, I have always been able to deal on my own with all the malfunctions of the body, and my relationship with it has in general been so close that it now looks as if the doctor had been inserted like a wedge into the familiar state of unity. A helping invader! Nonetheless, I was fortunate since I found a helper to whom I could soon speak as to a friend; we agreed to eliminate medication as much as possible and to see to it that nature, which for decades had proven itself to me as well meaning, was only slightly supported in its oscillations, which it apparently employs to achieve a new balance. I have never drawn clear boundaries between body and spirit and soul: one has served the other and affected the other, and each has been to me wonderful and pleasant. Thus, nothing seems more odd and strange to me than placing a superior, intellectual mind opposite a failing and sickly body. The dislike for doing so and my inability in this regard have as a consequence the fact that physical disturbances affect me more than others: was not everything at which I succeeded, even every insight, the result of the combined glad disposition of each of these elements, of their harmony?

Enough, I do not like to talk about all this and could hardly bear, as a sick person, to have someone else around me; at those times, a truly animal-like need of wanting to withdraw and hide governs all my moves. Here and now, I allowed myself to elaborate in such detail for once, and as an exception, because any other report that had been shorter and merely cursory would have destroyed the sense of my closeness that I wanted to convey to you on these sheets of paper.

At least you have recorded for me all the things that are pressing on you during these difficult days, your thoughts, desires, and fears, even though I cannot always promise a reply. (You can imagine the mountain of work and correspondence that has grown while I was absent or not capable of tackling it.) And at least I am informed; and the better, the more essential and warm my word can be when it will reach you again in certain intervals.

RMR.

Yes, for me it was a veritable miracle, after your letter before last, to see this new one, which is catching the lights that have since risen as with many small, happy mirrors! The lights seemed to me firmly implanted into the new foundation, so that I am hardly concerned with their course and progressive ascent into clarity. But I still think of you each day in hopes that you will remain under their influence and capable of following the waving of the new sky. And apart from that, you do not think that you are too generous by being so willing to change, accepting the nature of your fate, flowing into the unexpectedly open cast of a fully shaped future. Do you not sense behind the extreme possibilities of this obedience the one constant: a friendly and equally shy and daring submission? And what does living mean but this courage to fully grow into a cast, which one day will be broken off from our new shoulders, so that one can now, freed by this transformation, become acquainted with all the other creatures that have been magically placed into the same kingdom?

The way that you stood tall after so much measured and worthy achievement, humble and yet with a pure expectation to be somehow recognized, makes it impossible, it seems to me, that anything wrong could address and touch you: the voice that called certainly deserves to be trusted, deserves your open ear, deserves joy.

R.

In the introduction to each volume, English translations of direct quotations from the German are mine.

Letters on God

During the years of World War I (1914–18), Rilke lived in Munich, where he had attended the university years earlier, studying art, literature, and religion.

1. The addressee of this letter is Lotte Hepner. No letters of hers to Rilke are known to be extant.

2. Rilke's novel *The Notebooks of Malte Laurids Brigge* was published in 1910. It describes the reflections of a young Danish nobleman and poet living in Paris. In the bustling and noisy surroundings of city life, Brigge muses about his family and their history, death, love, and the meaning of life. For a time, Rilke had visited Denmark, studying Danish and reading Kierkegaard. Many of the themes and visual images that occur in Rilke's poetry are found and explored here.

3. Wilhelm Fliess (1858–1928) was a German otolaryngologist who practiced in Berlin. In 1887, Fliess attended several of Sigmund Freud's conferences in Vienna, and the two soon formed a friendship. Through their correspondence, Fliess came to play a leading role in the later development of psychoanalysis. He also developed a theory about a connection between the nose and the genitals and that of innate bisexuality, which Freud adopted. Fliess may have been among the first to formulate the concept of the biorhythm. For two years, Lou Andreas-Salomé had studied with Freud in Vienna. A student of the psychologist, she had introduced Rilke to Freud (in Munich) and to his theories and, by implication, to those of Fliess.

4. Leo Tolstoy (1828–1910) was a Russian writer and novelist. His *War and Peace* and *Anna Karenina* describe the breadth of nineteenth-century Russian life in concrete, realistic fashion. He was also known as an essayist, dramatist, and educational reformer. Following a conversion experience, he began interpreting the sayings of Jesus in more literal ways, especially the Sermon on the Mount, and became a fervent pacifist. He opposed private property and the institution of marriage,

and he practiced celibacy. His Christian interpretations and essays on celibacy, poverty, and nonviolent resistance influenced such pivotal figures of the twentieth century as Mohandas Gandhi and Martin Luther King Jr. Rilke had met Tolstoy in 1899 and 1900 when traveling in Russia.

5. Rilke initially had titled the letter "Remembering Verhaeren" ("Erinnerungen an Verhaeren"). Emile Verhaeren (1855–1916) was a Belgian poet, art critic, and author of short stories who wrote in French. Originally educated by the Jesuits, he later earned a law degree but then devoted his time to literature. By the turn of the century, he had won international acclaim for his poetry and writing. He was nominated for the Nobel Prize in Literature in 1911. His first collection of poems, *Les Flamandes,* was published in 1883 and had been inspired by Flemish paintings. Verhaeren described in a direct, naturalistic, and often provocative way his country and the Flemish people, which made a deep impression on the avant-garde but caused controversy and outrage in Roman Catholic circles. Rilke had met Verhaeren, who lived near Paris, in 1905 and admired his work greatly for its realism, clarity, and honesty. Verhaeren was killed when he accidentally fell under a train.

6. Assisi, Italy, was the birthplace and place of death of Saint Francis (1182–1226); it is situated on the southern hillside of Monte Subasio and offers a view onto the valley. In the third book of *The Book of Hours,* Saint Francis is featured prominently.

7. The fortresslike papal palace in Avignon had been erected in the fourteenth century. At the time, France reigned over the papacy, and all the popes between 1305 and 1378 were French. With that, the seat of the papacy had been moved from Rome to Avignon between 1309 and 1377. When the papacy moved its seat back to Rome, a French pope was elected regardless, residing at Avignon and opposing the one in Rome between 1378 and 1408.

8. The papal palace and the Gothic cathedral church, whose portal is presumed to be the remains of a temple to the Greek god Heracles (more familiarly known as Hercules, the name used by the Romans), sit atop a rocky plateau about 200 feet (60 meters) above the city.

9. A medicinal herb.

10. In the Mediterranean it was not uncommon for Christian churches to be built on top of pagan temples.

11. St. Eustache is at the south end of the Rue Montmartre and was built between 1532 and 1637. One of the most frequently visited churches of Paris, it offers good church music, especially on festival days.

12. Rilke probably meant Meaux, near Paris, with its unfinished cathedral, Saint-Étienne.

13. It is possible that Rilke is integrating autobiography here, since in 1911, he had met in Paris the seventeen-year-old Marthe Hennebert, who was a worker living in abject poverty. Rilke enlisted the help of friends to offer the lively girl, whom he considered his adopted daughter, an education and living quarters. They kept in touch until after the war years. In time, Hennebert married an artist and tapestry maker, and she had her own tapestry exhibits.

14. Possibly a reference to the famous glass paintings in the high church of Sainte-Chapelle in Paris; its fifteen windows and rose window depict more than a thousand scenes of biblical stories.

15. A Rhône island near Avignon.

Letters to a Young Woman

1. Prior to beginning a lecture tour through Switzerland that had allowed him to receive a visa to the country, Rilke stayed at an inn, the converted Palazzo Salis in Soglio, Switzerland, between July and September 1919.

2. Elvire Bachrach, the wife of a wealthy businessman, had offered Rilke a pavilion on the grounds of her chalet near Ascona. He decided to inspect the accommodations first by staying at the Grand Hotel in Locarno; finding them unacceptable, he moved to a small, modest pension, Villa Muralto, in Locarno in December 1919.

3. The tour, begun in Zurich as a rousing success, took Rilke also to St. Gall, Lucerne, Basel, Bern, and Winterthur. Up to six hundred people at a time were present at some of these lectures. The repertoire ranged from Rilke's early days in Schmargendorf (Berlin) and Worpswede through the Paris years and *New Poems,* along with his more recent work in religious and secular verse. Rilke also included reminiscences of Tolstoy, Rodin, and Verhaeren, whom he declared his important role models in regard to writing and poetry. Rilke had met Leo Tolstoy twice, in 1899 and 1900, during his Russia travels with Lou Andreas-Salomé; he had first met Rodin in 1902, served as his secretary for a while, and published a monograph on the sculptor in 1903; and he had met Verhaeren in 1905 and begun translating his poetry from French into German.

4. War broke out while Rilke was in Munich, and his belongings and books back in Paris, where he had been living for the past twelve years, were confiscated and auctioned off.

5. In 1920, Rilke had intended to spend the winter in Geneva and arrangements had been made, but then Nanny Wunderly left a message for him in Bern that a Colonel Richard Ziegler and his wife, Lily, were prepared to let him spend the winter at their château Berg, a spacious castle with parks in Canton Zurich. While at Berg, it became clear to Rilke that he wanted to live in Switzerland for the rest of his life.

6. The attraction of Wallis to Rilke was also that the canton was in the French-speaking part of Switzerland. On a weeklong vacation in October 1920, Rilke had visited Wallis with Baladine "Merline" Klossowska, a divorced painter. They had fallen in love the month before, and their deep relationship would endure to the end of Rilke's life. Unlike with his own daughter, Rilke took a lively interest in the education of Merline's sons, Pierre and Balthusz. Rilke saw to it that Balthusz's art was published when the boy was only thirteen. Balthusz (Balthus) became a world-renowned painter, Pierre a novelist and painter.

7. When in April 1921 Rilke was forced to leave Berg, Merline came from Berlin to help him look for a suitable place, another "Berg." Merline arrived in mid-June. She was the one to discover the small château Muzot. But negotiations faltered since the landlady wanted a year's rental commitment and Rilke was prepared for no more than three months. Nanny Wunderly, who was like a sister to Rilke, appealed to Werner Reinhart, her cousin and a Swiss merchant and arts benefactor, for help. Reinhart agreed to rent the place for a year and sublease it to Rilke for however long he wished, making him the castle's administrator. Merline, who helped renovate the quarters, stayed there with Rilke through November. In 1922, Reinhart bought Muzot to provide Rilke with a permanent residence. Rilke considered Merline the muse of the *Elegies*, which he wrote there.

8. The summer cottage that the women were leasing was not winterized, making conditions hard for the three of them.

9. Rilke uses the German word *Grabmal*, which means "gravestone," for what is translated here as "requiem." The girl was Wera Ouckama Knoop, who was a friend of Rilke's daughter, Ruth, during their Munich years. As a child Wera had been a dancer, but in light of an undiagnosed illness and the weight she gained on account of it, she devoted herself to playing the piano. She died at age nineteen of leukemia in 1919. Rilke resumed contact with the mother in 1921, informing her of Ruth's engagement. On January 1, 1922, Rilke received a package from the girl's mother, Gertrud Knoop: she had sent him her daughter's journal in which she had recorded her approaching death. This jour-

nal confronted Rilke with the death of a young person, prompting the outpouring of the *Sonnets to Orpheus* the same year. Ironically, it also confronted Rilke with the onset of the same illness as Wera's that would take his life four years later. Though Rilke began feeling ill in 1922 and went to stay at sanatoriums numerous times over the coming years, he never permitted his physician to tell him the diagnosis of his illness.

10. Albrecht Dürer (1471–1528) was a German painter and print-maker from Nuremberg. He also wrote several mathematical treatises. An advocate of Martin Luther's reforms in Germany, Dürer through his etchings, woodcuts, and lithographs contributed significantly to popularizing Protestant themes. Among his famous drawings are *The Hare, The Praying Hands,* the *Apocalypse* woodcuts, and *Saint Jerome in His Study.* Dürer's introduction of classical motifs into the art of Northern Europe through his knowledge of Italian artists and German human-ists, along with his elaborate prints and his novel printmaking process, made him one of the most important artists of the Renaissance in Northern Europe.

11. Referring to the *Duino Elegies,* which Rilke had completed on February 14, 1922.

Decker, Gunnar. *Rilkes Frauen oder Die Erfindung der Liebe.* Leipzig: Reclam Verlag, 2004.

Exner, Richard. Foreword and introduction to *Das Marienleben,* by Rainer Maria Rilke. Frankfurt: Insel Verlag, 1999.

Freedman, Ralph. *Life of a Poet: Rainer Maria Rilke.* Lyrical verse translated by Helen Sword in collaboration with the author. New York: Farrar, Straus, and Giroux, 1996.

Görner, Rüdiger. *Rainer Maria Rilke: Im Herzwerk der Sprache.* Vienna: Paul Zsolnay Verlag, 2004.

Holthusen, Hans Egon. *Rainer Maria Rilke: Mit Selbstzeugnissen und Bilddokumenten.* Hamburg: Rowohlt Verlag, 1958.

Kidder, Annemarie S. Introduction to *Pictures of God: Rilke's Religious Poetry, including "The Life of the Virgin Mary,"* by Rainer Maria Rilke. Translated by Annemarie S. Kidder. Livonia, Mich.: First Page Publications, 2005.

————. Introduction to *The Book of Hours: Prayers to a Lowly God,* by Rainer Maria Rilke. Translated by Annemarie S. Kidder. Evanston, Ill.: Northwestern University Press, 2001.

Kippenberg, Katharina. *Rainer Maria Rilke: Ein Beitrag.* Leipzig: Insel Verlag, 1935.

Koenig, Hertha. *Rilkes Mutter.* Tübingen: Neske Verlag, 1963.

Mandel, Siegfried. Introduction to *Visions of Christ: A Posthumous Cycle of Poems,* by Rainer Maria Rilke. Translated by Aaron Kramer. Boulder: University of Colorado Press, 1967.

Merton, Thomas. *Faith and Violence: Christian Teaching and Christian Practice.* Notre Dame, Ind.: University of Notre Dame Press, 1968.

Metzger, Erika A., and Michael M. Metzger. *A Companion to the Works of Rainer Maria Rilke.* Rochester, N.Y.: Camden House, 2001.

Nalewski, Horst. Afterword to *Briefwechsel mit einer jungen Frau,* by Rainer Maria Rilke. Edited by Horst Nalewski. Frankfurt: Insel Verlag, 2003.

Rilke, Rainer Maria. *Briefe an eine junge Frau.* Leipzig: Insel Verlag, 1930.

————. *Briefe an einen jungen Dichter.* Leipzig: Insel Verlag, 1929.

————. *Briefe an seinen Verleger 1906 bis 1926.* Edited by Ruth Rilke-Sieber and Carl Sieber. Leipzig: Insel Verlag, 1934.

————. *Werke: Kommentierte Ausgabe in Vier Bänden*. Edited by Manfred Engel, Ulrich Fülleborn, Horst Nalewski, and August Stahl. Frankfurt: Insel Verlag, 1996.

Rilke, Rainer Maria, and Lou Andreas-Salomé. *Briefwechsel*. Edited by Ernst Pfeiffer. Zurich: M. Niehaus, 1952.

Schnack, Ingeborg. *Rainer Maria Rilke: Chronik seines Lebens und seines Werkes*. 2 vols. Frankfurt: Insel Verlag, 1975.

Sieber, Carl. Afterword to *Briefe an eine junge Frau*, by Rainer Maria Rilke. Leipzig: Insel Verlag, 1930.

————. Foreword to *Über Gott: Zwei Briefe*, by Rainer Maria Rilke. Leipzig: Insel Verlag, 1933.